Naples, Florida

A PHOTOGRAPHIC PORTRAIT

PHOTOGRAPHY BY KAREN T. BARTLETT

Copyright © 2006 by
Twin Lights Publishers, Inc.

All rights reserved. No part of this book may be reproduced in any form without written permission of the copyright owners. All photographs are the property of Karen T. Bartlett, and no responsibility is accepted by producer, publisher, or printer for any infringement of copyright or otherwise arising from the contents of this publication. Every effort has been made to ensure that credits accurately comply with information supplied.

First published in the United States of America by:

Twin Lights Publishers, Inc.
8 Hale Street
Rockport, Massachusetts 01966
Telephone: (978) 546-7398
http://www.twinlightspub.com

ISBN: 1-885435-70-3
ISBN: 978-1-885435-70-5

10 9 8 7 6 5 4 3 2 1

Frontispiece:

Intracoastal Waterway

Opposite:

Endless Beach: A scene on Keewaydin Island

Karen T. Bartlett's photographs of:

Dale Chilhuly - *Red Chandelier,* 2000. Courtesy of the Naples Art Museum

Ernest Trova - *F/M6' Walking Jackman,* 1985 Courtesy of the Philharmonic Center for the Arts: Gift of the Wood Foundation

Editorial researched and written by:
Francesca and Duncan Yates
www.freelancewriters.us

Book design by:
SYP Design & Production, Inc.
www.sypdesign.com

Printed in China

In 1880, a man named Walter N. Haldeman owned virtually all of the land in present-day Naples. The sugar-white beaches were breathtaking, the sunrises surreal, and the fishing was the stuff of legends. Dense tangles of tropical vegetation covered nearly every inch of land. Haldeman predicted that Naples would become just as popular as Florida's east coast, and he was determined to hasten that awareness. Even though the entire community consisted of a cluster of small houses, Haldeman optimistically built a hotel and a 600-foot pier. As visitors experienced the tranquility and natural wonders of Southwest Florida, the region grew, establishing a loyal community of year-round and seasonal residents who defined Naples as not only home, but a piece of heaven.

Adjacent to the western entrance to the Everglades, in one of the world's last wild places, Naples has carved a world-class residential and resort haven out of the sub-tropical landscape. Known for its impressive waterside homes, championship golf resorts, cosmopolitan shopping venues and four-star restaurants, Naples is also blessed with a prolific art community that has transformed a sleepy fishing village into a top destination for national and international art collectors.

Naples' natural beauty and small-town semblance has attracted not only the retired or wealthy, but younger, middle-class families seeking a connection with nature as well as a sense of community.

Although much has changed in Naples since Haldeman lived here, some things—beaches, sunsets, fishing, and cool Gulf breezes—will always remain the same. Even the city pier is still here, now jutting 1,000 feet out into the Gulf—a symbol of one man's vision and a community's character and determination to persevere. Haldeman would, without a doubt, be proud of this modern tropical paradise called Naples.

PATH TO THE PIER

Rebuilt after a fire and ferocious hurricanes in 1910, 1926 and 1960, this thousand-foot fishing pier has come to symbolize the unwavering character and determination of the people of Naples. It is the last license free fishing pier in Florida.

FLY FISHING

Although fly fishing has been practiced here for over a century, it has grown in popularity in recent years. Local estuaries, creeks, and bays are home to a variety of game fish that are readily fooled by local anglers' well-tied flies. As one captain put it, *"The conditions in Naples are absolutely ideal for fly-fishing, but the good news is that the fish don't seem to know it yet."*

THE COLORS OF NAPLES *(above)*

Neapolitans take the color schemes of their homes from the colors of the sea and sky. The majority of homes reflect the subtle hues of sand, driftwood, sunsets and seashells.

DRIFTWOOD STATUARY *(opposite)*

Beach walkers along the more remote beaches of Naples are enchanted to come across natural driftwood formations, bleached over time by the sun and salty sea.

SHOWERS ON THE HORIZON *(opposite)*

Summertime in Naples is characterized by its sudden afternoon showers. They form swiftly out of a perfect cloudless sky, then disappear as fast as they came, washing the landscape in luminous sunshine once again.

A SPORT-FISHING PARADISE *(above)*

In the pristine blue-green waters at the northern delta of Wiggins Pass, where the Cocohatchee River meets the Gulf of Mexico, waters run deep, attracting larger game fish and enthusiastic sport fishermen.

LOWDERMILK BEACH PARK *(above)*

Colorful umbrellas dot the shoreline along Lowdermilk Beach Park's thousand-foot strip of white, sandy beach. Park patrons can enjoy a day in the sun, taking full advantage of picnic areas, a playground, and volleyball court.

IN MEMORIAM *(opposite)*

Leisure boaters and daytrippers have long enjoyed this charming landmark just off the coast of Naples, reminiscent of the quaint fish houses of the early 1900s. Originally built as a weekend cottage on the beach at Cape Romano, decades of shifting sands left it rising out of the shallow flats a few hundred feet off shore. Sadly, soon after this photograph was taken, the stilt house was swept away during Hurricane Wilma in October, 2005.

SEAGRAPES (opposite)

An abundance of seagrape plants can be found in Naples. Native to America's tropical seashores, it is a valuable, ornamental plant that brings rich green color to oceanside homes and protective support for dunes along treasured beaches.

COASTAL COMMUNITIES (top and bottom)

Native brown pelicans, ibis, herons, egrets and gulls are an iconic part of Florida's Gulf Coast. Old dock pilings and shoreline jetties serve as thrones for pelicans, while shore fowl lord over treasures at the water's edge.

HEAVENLY EXPERIENCE *(left)*

When the wind isn't right for sailing, it's perfect for parasailing. From a seagull's perspective, one may see dolphins, manatees, giant snook, schools of jellyfish and stingrays and giant loggerhead turtles just below the surface of the water.

WATERSPORT ENTHUSIAST *(right)*

Regardless of age, watersports, including sea kayaking, are a popular part of the local culture. The calm waterways and passes throughout Naples are ideal for novice and avid water enthusiasts alike.

PAILS OF PROMISE *(opposite)*

After an exciting day of building sandcastles, splashing, swimming, and shell-seeking, young beach goers retire for naps in the shade, while the pails left behind promise tomorrow's return.

AURA OF THE GULF (opposite)

Some afternoons along Clam Pass Beach, Gulf waters seem almost luminous and jade-like, like the shimmer of the aurora borealis in northern skies.

BEACH VOLLEYBALL (top)

After school and on weekends, young people gather at Lowdermilk Park and at the foot of the Naples Pier (pictured here) for serious exercise and lots of fun. Bystanders are often recruited, as are younger siblings.

CLAM PASS BEACH (bottom)

Three thousand feet of alabaster sand and a boardwalk that curves through a forest of mangrove trees and seagrapes are just a few reasons why Clam Pass was voted one of the top 20 beaches in the United States.

OSPREY (opposite)

Aptly called "fish hawks," these beautiful birds of prey can be found wherever there are fish. The shores, inlets and passes in and around Naples are a wonderland for ornithologists and bird-watching enthusiasts.

ALONG WIGGINS PASS (above)

The natural forest of mangroves along the Cocohatchee River provides nutrition for the marine animals that begin their life in the backwaters before entering the Gulf at Wiggins Pass.

"PEER" FISHING

The Naples Pier is a popular spot where local residents and visitors find camaraderie while enjoying a few hours of license-free fishing, courtesy of the City of Naples.

FOR FISHERMEN ONLY *(top)*

This section of the mile-long beach at Delnor-Wiggins Pass State Park prohibits swimmers, providing shore fishermen their own pristine oasis. Rated one of the best beaches in the country, swimming is allowed to the south.

FISHING IN THE PINK *(bottom)*

The shores along Wiggins Pass offer excellent fishing for both man and sea fowl. However, fishermen must be prepared to share their bait with an occasional egret.

ULTIMATE GETAWAY *(following page)*

The early riser is rewarded with the serenity and tranquility of the Gulf of Mexico and its deep-blue waters that color the far reaches of the still horizon.

SURF'S UP *(top)*

Dedicated surfers and skim-boarders impatiently wait for days when the surf's up along Naples beaches. Their passionate speed and fluid motion belie the practice behind their skill.

WAVE RUNNING *(bottom)*

The freedom of a personal water craft is a great way to explore Naples' inland waterways to catch a glimpse of a rich variety of wildlife—from egrets and gators to manatee and the rare Florida panther.

BEACH BALLET *(opposite)*

The beauty and inspiration of the Gulf seas and sand are expressed in a dancer's joyous movement. Each day cool, morning air and late afternoon breezes draw walkers, runners and yoga enthusiasts to the beach.

MORNING ALONG PARK SHORE *(top)*

Changing tides leave stretches of pools that reflect the morning light. Access to the tranquility of the beach for an early-morning jog or long walk is one of the many charms of the lovely Park Shore section of the city.

LOWDERMILK SOLITUDE *(bottom)*

Soft azure and pink skies signal the beginning of a perfect Naples morning. Quiet at dawn, the beach will soon echo with the laughter of children and the scent of tanning lotion.

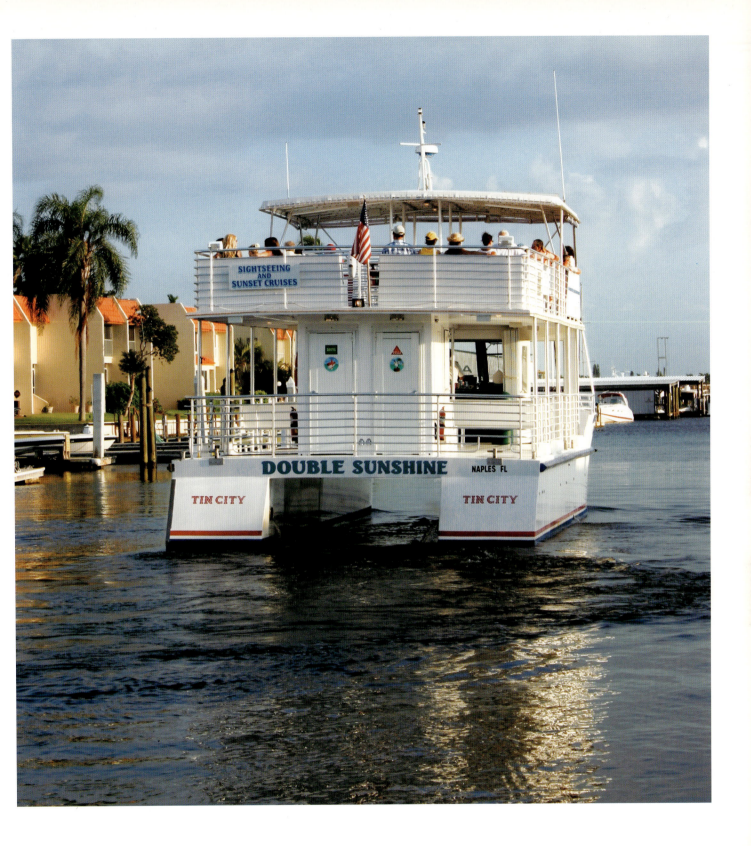

A DAY FOR A CRUISE

Often accompanied by dolphins and manatees that frolic close by, the tour boat *Double Sunshine* departs from Tin City, providing passengers a relaxing way to view daily shoreline activity.

SUNSET RITUAL

When the sun begins to sink below the horizon, Neapolitans gather on the beach, like an instinctive, ancient migration. Toasting fiery Gulf sunsets is a cherished ritual here in paradise, like having front-row seats at a grand, theatrical event.

BLAZING SUNSET

Naples Pier reaches out over the Gulf waters providing a panoramic view of an amazing sunset over the Gulf of Mexico. This well-known link between land and sea is the fifth incarnation of the historic pier that was originally built in 1888.

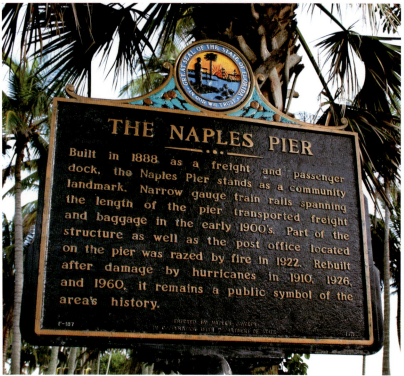

GOLDEN GULF SUNSET *(top)*

The lull of the waves combined with the dazzling colors of the sun's last rays can be mesmerizing. Sunsets all along Florida's Gulf coast are known as some of the most beautiful in the world.

LOCAL LANDMARK *(bottom)*

Historic Naples Pier was a bustling, freight and passenger dock at the turn of the 19th century, with narrow-gauge train rails running the length of it, transporting freight and luggage. Today, the pier is a public symbol of Naples' history.

AN EVENING'S CATCH *(opposite)*

Silhouetted against a sunset sky, this fisherman casts his seine net out once more for tiny silver bait fish that may just lure "the big one."

RED SKIES AT NIGHT *(previous page)*

A spectacular sunset lights up the waves crashing on a Naples beach. Each wave sprinkles the sand with a bounty of seashells, waiting to be discovered at low tide by eager, early-morning shell hunters.

PICTURESQUE BOAT HOUSES *(above)*

A charming slice of early Naples is the double row of boat houses at the end of Gordon Drive. These tiny wooden structures, overlooking the Intracoastal Waterway, have been buffeted by storms over half a century, and yet, still stand.

HOME ON GORDON PASS *(top)*

Gordon Pass is home to one of Naples' most elegant waterfront communities, where homes and estates are individually designed and landscaped, each one more spectacular than the next.

GORDON PASS WATERWAY *(bottom)*

Of the three major Naples waterways out to the Gulf, Gordon's Pass is the furthest south. A short scenic ride brings boaters to Naples Bay, Keewaydin and Marco Islands, and the mysterious Ten Thousand Islands and the northern tip of the Everglades.

PELICAN BAY (above)

Bordered by miles of pristine Gulf beachfront, the Pelican Bay community is comprised of a variety of luxury home designs, as well as a natural preserve with 40 acres of parks and nature trails.

VANDERBILT BEACH (opposite)

Adjacent to the luxurious resorts, shopping and dining experiences of Pelican Bay, Vanderbilt Beach is known for its beautiful sunsets and quiet, relaxed atmosphere, amidst graceful palm trees.

NAPLES MUSEUM OF ART *(opposite)*
Sculpture *Homeward Bound* ©: Anna Marie Houser

Affiliated with the Philharmonic Center for the Arts, this is Southwest Florida's first full-scale art museum. Extensive collections in fifteen galleries include modern Mexican art and works by American masters from 1900–1955.

DALE CHIHULY'S RED CHANDELIER, 2000 *(above)*

The centerpiece of the Figge Conservatory at the Naples Museum of Art, this magnificent tentacled glass form is an imposing 244 x 144 x 144 inches in size and stimulates the imagination with its lifelike energy.

41

PUBLIC ART *(above)*

The enchantment of Naples is due in no small part to its wealth of outdoor art; not just on the grounds of museums and galleries but gracing private gardens, city streets, shopping plazas and restaurants.

IN FLIGHT *(opposite)*

The Neapolitan love for the arts, reflected in the city's numerous galleries, museums, and music venues, is on par with their esteem for native wildlife.

MAN AND NATURE AS ART

One of Naples' most exclusive shopping areas is Third Street South. Residents and vistiors come to browse through the many antique shops, art galleries, designer boutiques and compelling sidewalk statuary.

GALLERY ROW

Naples has quickly become one of the country's top art destinations. Situated in elegant Old Naples, Gallery Row is home to many galleries where one can find the works of Old Masters as well as those of emerging artists.

PHILHARMONIC CENTER FOR THE ARTS

The "Phil," as locals fondly call it, is the premier performing arts venue in Southwest Florida. It hosts over 400 events each year, including classical and popular music, Broadway musicals and world-class opera and dance.

ERNEST TROVER'S WALKING JACKMAN

Ernest Trover's *FM/6 Walking Jackman*, 1985, stainless steel (ed.2/9) is the striking focal point at the entrance to the Philharmonic Center for the Arts. The sculpture stands 110 x 180 x 180 inches. The Phil offers visual and performing arts, including a resident symphony orchestra, as well as outreach and educational programs for the community.

ST. KATHERINE'S (above)

Organized in 1985, St. Katherine's Greek Orthodox Church is a relatively young parish. The architectural design of the church reflects a Mediterranean influence that is so much a part of Naples. The church's new sanctuary opened in 2002.

ST. WILLIAM BELL TOWER (opposite)

The patina on the copper bell tower of the St. William Catholic Church belies the brief history of this congregation. Begun in 1973, members first met in a local school. As the parish grew, the present church was built, opening in 1980.

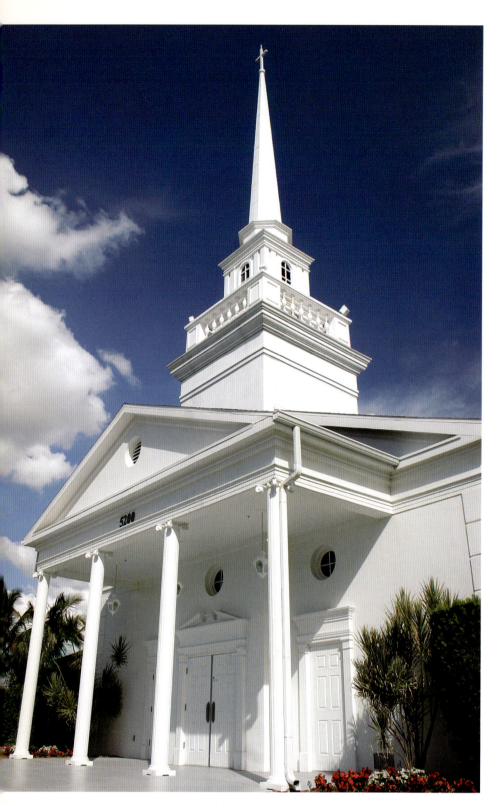

NAPLES UNITED CHURCH OF CHRIST

The traditional lines and spire of the Naples United Church of Christ, located in the Seagate neighborhood, reflects the 17th-century New England roots of the religious denomination that formed when German and English sects united.

TRINITY-BY-THE-COVE

One of the most beautiful small churches in Florida, Trinity-by-the-Cove Episcopal Church is tucked among the mansions of Port Royal, surrounded by lush lawns and Royal Palms.

A PASSION FOR TENNIS *(above)*

Tennis is more than a casual pastime for many Neapolitans. Private tennis clubs, associated with the area's planned communities, support a strong network of men's, women's and doubles league teams.

GREAT WHITE HERON *(opposite)*

The majestic Great White Heron, among the most graceful and beautiful of the large sea birds, can be sighted deep in the mangroves, fishing along the tide line, and even strolling majestically across a freshly-mowed lawn.

HISTORIC TROLLEY TOURS

A trolley tour is a fun and comfortable way to see the many attractions and neighborhoods of Naples. Naples Trolley Tours excite tourists with a unique, two-hour drive in a replica 1907 "Cincinnati, Ohio" trolley.

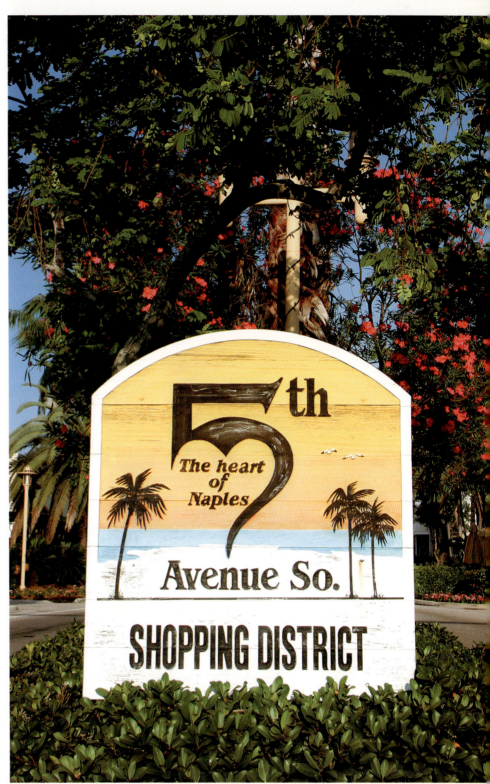

FIFTH AVENUE SOUTH

True to its name, Fifth Avenue South gives shoppers a luxurious experience in a resort setting. Ending at the beach, this broad tree-lined street has fashionable shops, galleries and European bistros.

MEDITERRANEAN ELEGANCE

Naples' Fifth Avenue South offers shoppers more than upscale fares. Visitors experience traditional South Floridian architecture and style with its Mediterranean influence, from palm-lined walkways to courtyards with splashing fountains and shaded seating under tropical foliage or umbrellas. The elegant shop façades open to galleries, jewelers, Italian shoe or designer dress boutiques.

VON LIEBIG ART CENTER *(top and bottom)*

Begun in 1954 as an outdoor painting group of local artists, this community arts center, named for surgical textiles inventor, William von Liebig and his wife Suzanne, has evolved into a dynamic cultural resource. The center offers art classes and free exhibitions of contemporary American art, with a focus on Florida artists. In 1998, the Naples Art Association announced the formation of a permanent art collection to celebrate the artistic legacy of this unique region of Florida.

A CITY OF FOUNTAINS *(opposite)*

Like her namesake in Italy, Naples pays tribute to water in all its forms. The soothing sounds of fountains can be heard at the entrances to residential communities, shopping centers, and on random walls like this one at The Village on Venetian Bay.

THIRD STREET SOUTH SHOPS *(above)*

Located in Old Naples, the quaint Third Street gallery and shopping area features many restored, early 20th-century structures, including "Cracker Style" cottages, with their open windows, verandas and cupolas designed to let in cooling breezes.

GALLERY ROW MERMAID *(opposite)*

Outside of the Galerie du Soleil on Naples' distinguished Gallery Row, a mermaid sits on the curb, pondering the ongoing activity. Numerous fine-art galleries have made Naples a nationally ranked art market.

BAYFRONT MARINA

The marina at Bayfront provides a link between the blue waters around Naples and upscale dining and shopping at this lovely waterside oasis located at the east end of Fifth Avenue South.

BRIGHT AND BREEZY

The charm and elegance of "Old World" Naples is inherent in the façades and brick walkways that make up the multi-use Bayfront area. Residential condominiums offer breathtaking views of Naples Bay and beyond.

THE RED CARPET

The jewel in the Ritz Carlton crown, the Five Diamond rated Ritz Carlton Beach Resort delivers the ultimate experience in luxury, including a world-class spa and a variety of exceptional restaurants on the premises.

VELVET GREENS

The Ritz Carlton Golf Resort offers stunning views and extensive amenities including the famous greens of Naples' Tiburon Golf Club. One of the finest golf resorts in Florida, its 36 holes were designed by golfing great Greg Norman.

LONE GULL

A solitary seabird lights upon a weathered piling to model the crisp clean lines of his colorful feathers. The Naples waterfront is teeming with beautiful winged species of all kinds.

WATERWAYS OF NAPLES

Communities along the inlets and bights of land within Inner Doctors Bay and Venetian Bay enjoy extensive waterfront real estate and parks as well as protection from the open Gulf of Mexico to the west.

OLD-WORLD GRANDEUR

The afternoon light illuminates the courtly architecture of these seaside residences at The Strand community in North Naples.

GATHERING AT SUNRISE

At sunrise, shore birds search the water's edge for delicacies left by the tide. Throughout Southwest Florida, ibis, egrets, heron, and wood storks can be seen roosting in mangroves, or wading in roadside canals and at the edges of pristine lakes.

OUT FOR A SPIN *(above)*

Pelican Bay, with its scenic, winding boulevard and gracious neighborhoods, is a favorite route for serious cycling clubs. Groups of a dozen or more in colorful attire can be seen gliding along in perfect tandem just after sunrise.

MIRRORED PALMS *(opposite)*

One does not have to be an avid golfer to appreciate the manicured greens and stately palms at the legendary Naples Beach Hotel and Golf Club, although it might require a non-golfer to appreciate the beauty of this water hazard.

IMAGINATIONS WELCOME (top)

Children love this fairyland playground of castle towers and turrets at the Cambier Park Playground in Old Naples. The park also has a performing arts stage and professional tournament courts with viewing stands.

THE WAKE DANCER (bottom)

Playful dolphins are beloved members of Naples' seaside communities. Frolicking alongside boats, most of these powerful mammals prefer to make friends from a distance.

GREAT BLUE HERON (opposite)

This shy heron, in his majestic breeding plumage, was captured by the photographer's lens in the back-country just south of Naples at the tip of the Everglades.

A VIBRANT HABITAT *(top)*

Passers-by get a special view of this historic guest cottage that is usually fenced for privacy when not being painted.

COTTAGES ON 8th STREET *(bottom)*

These new cottages of Old Naples reflect the easy-going lifestyle of an earlier time. Paned windows let in the sunshine and cool breezes. Fine architectural details make each home unique.

FAMILY TIES

Naples' residents take great pride in sharing the city's many sights and activities with visiting friends and family. The Naples Depot Museum, with its ride-on train and historic exhibits, is a favorite for all ages.

NAPLES CONCERT BAND (above)

For over 30 years, this all-volunteer band has entertained Neapolitans with old fashioned Sunday afternoon concerts in the bandshell at Old Naples' Cambier Park. Every year, the organization awards scholarships to participating students.

FLOURISHING CREATIVITY (opposite)

Outdoor art shows are a regular event on the streets of downtown Naples. In just 50 years, this city has evolved into a passionate artistic community that attracts serious art collectors from all over the world.

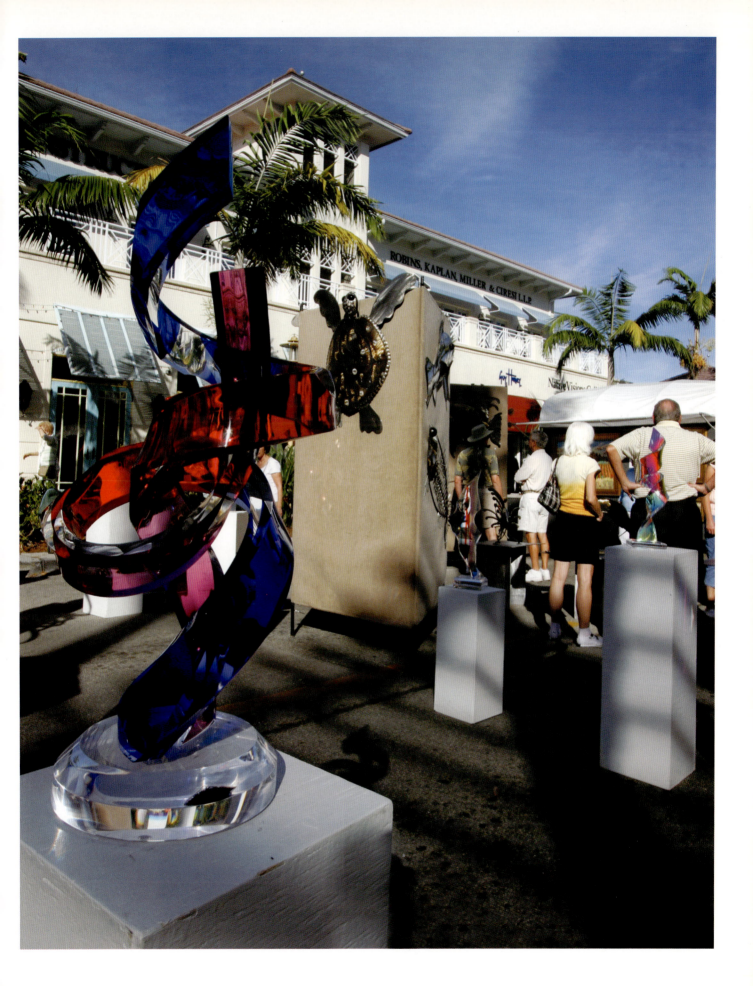

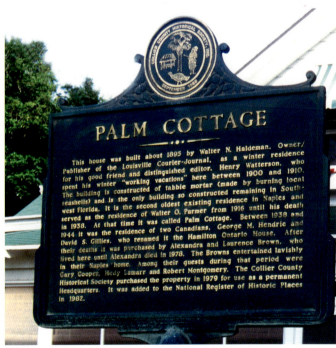

STRIKE UP THE BAND *(opposite)*

Everyone loves a parade, and one of the most popular features of Naples' parades is Barron Collier High School's nationally acclaimed marching band. The band, with its cutting-edge drum line and choreography, has performed internationally.

PALM COTTAGE *(top and bottom)*

Built in 1895, this historic house museum is operated by the Naples Historical Society. It is the second oldest house in Naples and is a fine example of tabby mortar construction, where mortar is made from a burnt mix of sand and seashells.

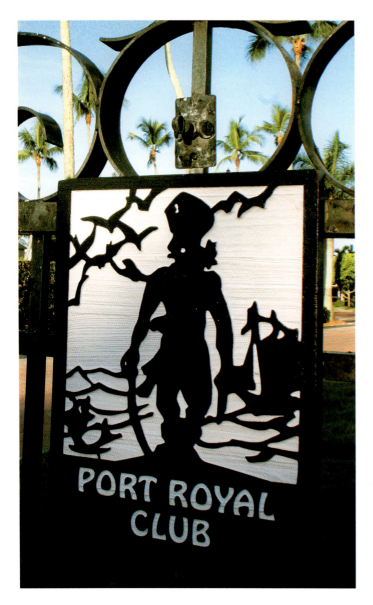 

WROUGHT-IRON ARTISTRY (left)

Local artisans take pride in creating some of the most elegant and unique railings, fences, and signage evident in public and private parks as well as residences throughout Naples.

FLORIDA PEACH (right)

The glorious colors and species variety of flowering hibiscus that thrive on Naples' sunshine, are a part of city parks and residential landscapes all over the city.

GATOR JAWS (opposite)

Florida is home to over a million alligators. Seen in the briny river outlets from Naples to the Everglades, they prefer fresh water to salt. The difference between an alligator and a crocodile is, if the bottom teeth are visible with a closed jaw, it's a crocodile.

TROMPE L'OEIL

Mural art, from grand-scale and spectacular to small and colorful, is among the treasures of this chic seaside town.

SIDEWALK BISTROS

European ambience is reflected in the many sidewalk cafés like this one on Third Street South. Campiello, with its ivy covered walls, wrought-iron balconies, umbrellas and a marble bar, is a popular spot to "see and be seen."

NIGHT AT THE DOCK

The lights on the tour boat, *Double Sunshine*, give the docks at Tin City a romantic glow. While laughter and music from local restaurants fill the air, the docks remain quiet but for the gentle lapping of water on still hulls.

TIN CITY

This cluster of quaint and colorful shacks dates back to the 1920's, when clam and oyster fishermen used the docks to process their catch. Now home to seafood restaurants and gift shops, it is a popular place to shop for souvenirs and curiosities.

EVENING ALONG FIFTH AVENUE

An air of casual elegance sets the stage for an evening along Old Naples' Fifth Avenue South. Restaurants offer Asian, European and American cuisine, adding an international flair to this Gulf Coast community.

SUGDEN COMMUNITY THEATER

This state-of-the-art playhouse became home to the Naples Players when it opened in 1998. Offering dramatic and musical productions, its volunteer staff of over 600 is a testament to Neapolitans' love for the theatre.

DINNER CRUISE *(top)*

The twinkling lights on the deck set a festive mood for what promises to be a night to remember, as guests enjoy a gourmet dinner and toast the setting sun, awash in golden hues.

REGINA'S ON FIFTH *(bottom)*

A jewel-colored neon sign lights up the warm evening air outside of Naples' oldest ice-cream parlor. The soft glow invites patrons to cool off with a double-scoop ice cream cone or authentic milk shake at an old-fashioned soda fountain.

STONE CRAB PICNIC *(opposite)*

Once a small fishing village, Naples has grown into a bustling resort city where vacationers and locals alike enjoy such delicacies as sweet, succulent stone crab claws dripping with hot, melted butter.

SOUTH FLORIDA GOLD

These stone crab claws are on their way to becoming a tasty item on Kelly's mouth-watering menu. Naples' stone crab is revered in exclusive restaurants where even the most refined patrons can enjoy eating with their fingers.

KELLY'S AND TIN CITY

Built in 1952 on the banks of the Gordon River, Kelly's Fish House is the oldest seafood restaurant in Naples. The original Kelly's was built in 1927 in South Boston.

NAPLES CITY DOCK *(above)*

At dawn, the light pinging of rigging against masts is interrupted by the eager voices and preparation of charter fishing boat captains and the fishermen who hope to catch the "big one" in the deep, Gulf waters.

SAILBOATS AT CITY DOCK *(opposite)*

City Dock welcomes boaters and pedestrians to its marina jutting out into Crayton Cove, with slips big enough for 120-foot yachts. With easy access to the Gulf of Mexico, Naples is a great starting point for a breezy sail.

JESSE AT CITY DOCK *(left)*

Walking along the City Dock must be a fascinating experience for Jesse. With his keen sense of smell, he can take in the salty breezes, the freshly caught fish, and the exotic aromas that escape from dockside restaurants.

COLLIER COUNTY FLAG *(right)*

The Collier County flag flutters in the gentle breeze with Old Glory. In 1888, the Naples Company came to Collier County bringing visitors from the north to hunt wild turkeys that roamed throughout the region. Hence the turkey on the flag.

VISITING SCHOONER *(opposite)*

Pleasure boats from all over cruise to the clear Gulf waters of Naples. With so much boating activity, local wildlife preservation groups work tirelessly to heighten safety awareness.

IBIS AT ST. THOMAS (above)

The tiny lake at St. Thomas in Pelican Bay is the home of an active seabird rookery. White ibis, with their dramatic, curved orange beaks, share the rookery with cormorants, herons, egrets, and their protector, one large gator.

LUSH AND BRILLIANT FLORA (opposite)

The graceful curving walls, subtle lighting and a sea of flowers surrounding this high rise in North Naples reflects the ambience of a community that reveres both privacy and the work of gifted landscape architects.

"BARONESS VON GATOR" (left)

Local artists were sponsored by area businesses to create these sculptures of vivacious personality to promote "Gators Galore," a fund-raising auction to benefit the Boys and Girls' Clubs of Naples and the Naples Art Association.

ARTS AND FLOWERS (right)

Ceramic mosaics grace the landscape of the recently established Naples Botanical Garden. A fully accredited living museum, the gardens are a center for natural science, plant collections, art, history exhibitions, and education.

"CHILI GATOR"

Brightly colored alligators strike humorous poses for passersby along the streets of Naples. The "Gators Galore" art exhibit produced sixty-five of these light-hearted reptiles that bring color and joy to the community.

RIPE FOR THE PICKIN'

December through April are harvesting months for these red, juicy berries in Naples. Pick your own, buy them at a roadside stand, or enjoy them in a scrumptious dessert at one of Naples' fine gourmet restaurants.

RUBY REDS

The citrus growers around Naples have spoiled their neighbors with yearly harvests of juicy and delectable oranges, grapefruits and tangerines. The sweet taste of Ruby Reds makes this richly colored grapefruit a favorite.

BANANA BLOSSOM (above)

The next time you peel a banana, think about the fact that you are about to eat an ancient fruit that has been cultivated for nearly 3,000 years. Some banana trees grow twenty feet high.

ROYAL POINCIANA (opposite)

Native to Madagascar, the Royal Poinciana in bloom are breathtaking. For about eight weeks each summer, Naples is ablaze with a glorious show of Royal Poinciana trees. After their peak, blossoms drop, creating a lush red blanket on the ground below.

SNAPDRAGONS *(above)*

Asians call this lush flower "rabbit's lips" and the Dutch nickname it "lion's lips." Americans prefer "snapdragons" because when you squeeze the blossom, it opens in the shape of a mythical dragon's snout.

WATER LILY *(opposite)*

The beauty of the water lily pond in early morning is just one of many floral delights awaiting visitors at the Naples Zoo at Caribbean Gardens. The historic botanical gardens were here fifty years before the animals arrived at the zoo.

SURREAL SUNSET *(above)*

Watching a sunset in Naples can be a religious experience. No two are ever the same. While some produce a glorious fireball, others reflect an afterglow of striking pinks, or shades that blend and peacefully dissolve into the evening sky.

BLUES *(opposite)*

A thunderhead stands at attention over a peaceful horizon. So much of Naples' scenery is extrodinarily artful, as this monochromatic image of blue on blue beautifully conveys.

FARMER'S MARKET *(above)*

The stands at the Saturday market behind the Plaza on Third Street are filled with fresh, locally-grown fruits and vegetables, as well as artwork, jams and jellies, and flowers. These farm-fresh purple zebra eggplants are as beautiful as they are delicious.

THE MYSTICAL BANYAN *(opposite)*

The massive banyan trees of Naples have a wonderful mythology. Indigenous to Asia, they are sacred to Hindus as they represent eternal life. It is said that if a wish is made at a banyan tree, it will most likely be granted.

INTO THE GULF *(opposite)*

The northwestern location of Wiggins Pass affords a wonderful vantage point for sunsets and outstanding fishing in the unusually deep waters just outside this delta.

HIBISCUS PATHWAY *(above)*

Naples Botanical Garden cultivates over 600 plant species in seven distinct, natural habitats and ecosystems. Plans are underway to expand the garden into one of the world's finest collections of tropical and sub-tropical plants.

CONSERVANCY BOAT RIDE *(top)*

Surrounded by mangroves, tropical plants and birds, the Gordon River is a great place to observe wildlife. A conservancy naturalist can point out the many fascinating aspects of this watery ecosystem while on a guided tour.

NATURE SEEKERS *(bottom)*

Hike the many wooded trails that loop through the 14-acre Conservancy Nature Center or enjoy a slow canoe ride on calm waterways. The abundance of wildlife here is awe-inspiring.

LOGGERHEAD HATCHLING *(opposite)*

This tiny hatchling begins his long journey out to sea. Naples' beaches are fertile nesting grounds for giant loggerhead turtles, who, year after year, return each spring to lay up to 100 eggs in the sand. Only one in ten thousand survives its first month of life.

KAYAKERS AT THE PASS

The serenity of an early morning on the sparkling coastal waters is interrupted only by the slight splash of canoe or kayak paddles.

PLUMERIA

When the sun goes down in Naples, the air is infused with the romantic fragrances of night-blooming jasmine and plumeria, that mix with the sultry, salt breezes of the Gulf.

THE GREEN GAME

It's claimed that Southwest Florida has more golf holes per capita than anyplace else in North America. Naples is a mecca for golfers with over 100 challenging, top-notch courses. Many of these well-manicured courses are part of luxurious golfing communities where homes and condominums overlook the fairways. Others have earned a coveted top ranking and attract serious golfers from around the world.

ORCHID

Orchids grow wild in the Everglades and are cultivated in residential gardens. The Naples Beach Hotel and Golf Resort developed its own ambitious Orchid Program, complete with a full-time horticulturist and over 5,000 plants.

GREENS KEEPER

"Birdie" takes on a different meaning at this Naples golf course where a solitary great white heron wanders onto the fairway.

MANGROVE ROOKERY (previous page)

Naples' Rookery Bay is nationally recognized as one of the few undisturbed mangrove estuaries remaining in the country. When fish food supplies are limited in winter, the mangroves fill with an amazing variety of pelicans, roseate spoonbills, ibis, herons, egrets, hawks, ospreys and bald eagles. This pristine site is part of one of the largest mangrove systems in North America and serves as an outdoor classroom and laboratory for students.

IBIS IN FLIGHT (above)

In winter months, the skies above Naples, Marco Island, and the Everglades fill with migratory birds, while flocks of birdwatchers below point binoculars and cameras skyward to capture these perfect moments.

PELICAN ROMANCE

There are countless opportunities to watch the unique rituals of birds around the waterways of Naples. Undisturbed, pelicans can build thousands of nests in mangrove rookeries, raising one to three chicks per nest each year.

BROWN PELICAN CAMEO

The brown pelican is common to the shores and mangrove-edged inlets around Naples. This species is the only dark pelican and the only one that plunges directly into the sea to catch prey with its great pocketed bill.

SNOWY EGRET

Naples lies directly in the path of one of the world's most-traveled flyways for migrating birds. More than 200 species have been spotted throughout the years. For many tourists, bird-watching is the best reason to travel to Naples.

OLEANDER BLOSSOMS *(opposite)*

A favorite with gardeners, Naples is replete with these luxuriant flowering trees in summer. Often fragrant, the flowers blossom in white, pink, red or yellow petals, against deep-green leaves. While lovely to view, their oils irritate the skin.

EXOTIC FIRE *(above)*

The wild and exotic beauty of the tropical trees and foliage of Naples is captured in the fiery petals of this vibrant bloom. Some species bloom all year long, decorating the Paradise Coast with color and life.

Photography by Stefan   www.CatchlightStudio.com

KAREN T. BARTLETT

Karen T. Bartlett is an award-winning professional photojournalist whose travel articles and photography appear regularly in magazines, travel guides, newspapers and books throughout North America and the Caribbean. Since leaving the corporate world—she spent nearly 20 years at the helm of a leading Atlanta public relations firm—her assignments have taken her from the savannas of South Africa to the temples of Bali, and from the medieval cities of Tuscany to the jungles of Belize. She has photographed the eerie castle ruins of the Marquis de Sade in the South of France, and descended into a teeming alligator pit at the edge of the Everglades. She has been interrogated in South Africa for traveling with a Zulu spear and has dined on live termites in Venezuela's Orinoco Delta. She went deep-sea fishing with former U.S. president Jimmy Carter, and she earned a reindeer driver license in Finland. She recently documented the primitive land-diving rituals on remote Pentecost Island in the South Pacific, and she has covered both indigenous and luxurious spa therapies from the marble palaces of Asia to the Dead Sea.

Karen lives in Naples, where she is a contributing editor of *Gulfshore Life* magazine. Her bylines and photography have appeared consistently in the region's leading magazines for the past decade. Her credentials also include the *Toronto Star*, *Caribbean Travel & Life* magazine, *N, The Magazine of Naples* and the book *The Best Florida Getaways*.

Karen is a member of ASMP, the American Society of Media Photographers and SATW, the Society of American Travel Writers. Many of the photographs featured in this book are available as hand-signed note cards and matted prints.

For more information about Karen, visit her website at www.karentbartlett.com.